HALF-LIFE OF EMPATHY

HALF-LIFE OF LIFE OF EMPATHY

REBECCA A. DURHAM

new RIVERS PRESS MSUM

Library of Congress Control Number: 2019956967
ISBN: 978-0-89823-394-0

New Rivers Press is a nonprofit literary press associated with Minnesota State University Moorhead.

Cover and interior design by Samantha Albrecht
Author photo by Emaline Aspen
The publication of *Half-life of Empathy* is made possible by the generous support of Minnesota State University Moorhead, the Dawson Family Endowment, and other contributors to New Rivers Press.

NRP Staff: Nayt Rundquist, Managing Editor; Kevin Carollo, Editor; Travis Dolence, Director; Trista Conzemius, Art Director
Interns: Gabbie Brandt, Dana Casey, Alex Ferguson, Katie Martinson, Delaney Noe, Olivia Rockstad

Half-life of Empathy book team: Gabbie Brandt, Jaeda Engberg, Andrew Reed

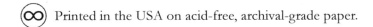 Printed in the USA on acid-free, archival-grade paper.

Half-life of Empathy is distributed nationally by Small Press Distribution.

 New Rivers Press
c/o MSUM
1104 7th Ave S
Moorhead, MN 56563
www.newriverspress.com

TABLE OF CONTENTS

I. HYPEROBJECTS

II. MEANDER BELT

III. LESS, UNLESS

An object, according to our understanding of hyperobjects, consists precisely of a rift between its appearance and its essence.

— TIMOTHY MORTON

but you are not a clean rain
and you are not pristine
but still we are together extremely wide tidal zone
shallow near shore waters
do you think we can stand it?

— JULIANA SPAHR

HYPEROBJECTS

IMAGINE BEING PRESENT
AND FINDING YOURSELF GONE

So present you
become dissolute.

No more body
than a leaf is sky.

The only duality,
a parting of sound.
Ears make your *I*.

Filling like
glacial till, ice pressed.
Scoured out, smoothed.

Now words fall
like budscales.
What follows?

INTO THE BIRDLESS ETHER

I. BODY AS HYPEROBJECT

My skin, a strata of pine
shed ochre, soles
of my feet graze
the ground like red
flashes of the pileated's
crest. Hands, cedar roots.
My voice a glissade, one
ruby-crowned kinglet.

Enough.
Enough you say.
Enough with
the naming of things.

What about the slow violence
charnel grounds . . . place
of life . . . of death-in-life
junk DNA . . . cyanide . . . radiation
. . . demonic forces . . . pollution?

Horsetail strobili
hold spore mother
cells. I drink
from the river
hands cupped.

I invite inoculation.
My lips are where the water is.

II. ECOMELANCHOLIA

As the Pacific Ocean warms, it heats
proteins, nudges the virus to life.

Sea stars shed limbs
fragmentation of body then death.

Populations plummet.

Sea stars   memory of salt limbs
sea stars   *known only from*
sea stars your absence leaves me

sea star *sharp decline*
sea star little resiliency

sea star the slack tide of you

rituals of burial
rituals of mourning

sea stars when we

seldom if ever

sea stars *less, unless*

III. AN EXQUISITE CREVASSE
MAY SWALLOW YOU

The air is entombed
and we are entombed
and a howl swells in me

but if stricken here held
by this insidious concrete
it must mean I am dead
and have no body
to scream with.

There is no air but from machines.
There are no birds, not even a shadowed
hint, or hum. There is nothing green.

We feed our hollowness.
Some cry or bicker.

Our ecology falters,
then fails, rudely forced
from true.

IV. COTTONWOOD SALVE

I am a gatherer now, or
have always been a gatherer.

Remember, maybe two hands.
Remember, a name

is not a lining of boundary.
Find the bud scales with the hard

caps intact. The blood-red resin
beads at its base. I gather half

a jar before I understand
what they held: yellow pollen

from purple anthers, or
nascent crimson cotton.

Wind stirs a charm of finches
from the branches. They loosen

more bud scales, and I glean
the spring-soaked husks. Together

we form a colony of entropy.
I reach and reach and resin stains.

BIOLOGICAL ASSESSMENT

I make gestures of thriving.
Start with what I know, kneeling.

Cells spun in long hollow strands.
Held together, this dance into form.

Beside it more lichen, blue green algae in there
breathing light. I make gestures of belonging.

I know between fallen leaves there's more
lichen and moss and turkey tail mushrooms

I know their action *will harm sensitive, threatened,
or endangered lichens and/or their habitats.*

Kneel here to memory, grey green, soon slain.

THE TEMPLE WILL SEE YOU NOW

In the temple of sunflowers
petals do not waver with breath

In the temple of sunflowers nothing
is found wanting, wanted, or wan

In the temple of sunflowers
disc flowers angle with ochre incisions

In the temple of sunflowers
birds scissor up green folds

In the temple of sunflowers
bees seize anyone who screams

In the temple of sunflowers
sunflowers mock the sun

IF WE ARE LOST
IN THE FOREST WE STAY STILL

hold our position
in the labyrinthine center
       (waxing north)

ericaceous faces upturn
       (fecundity holds)

mimulus
map yellow nebula
in their spotted throats

our fovea centralis
herds this, hears this
so we hoard light

a mist separates
in stellate hairs

spindle fibers
tease us

apart

I'M READY TO TELL YOU
ABOUT THE BODIES

I brought the bones of my own
but not theirs. Metal and belongings
bringing them planar with or without pollen.
All wings and thorax and mandibles
made flat. A smattering of mouths
and mounts in stillness across arbitrary ends
of Montana Idaho Washington
Oregon and California. I'm collecting
bodies in lines and lining large
and small splats with sculpted chitin.
The carved scales of damselflies
and split adders and beetles and bees
and the bodies of pests and pets.
A cemetery near the intake and I hit
the button to recirc what's recirculating.
What about these bodies flashing black.
Bodies across a distance walking
would take days and mean no bodies.
Bodies upset and past.

AS FOR THE BIRCH

death like that
leaves upturned
and the browning
her eyes say
this pale blue
enough to
shush the asters
sing wind like that
mere matter
the asking
of color of life
bracts between fingers
what stays
she says
enough, entropy is
everything, or at least
so much becoming
petioles spinning
enough to gather
she says
leaflessness
wild like that
wresting to let go

REDSTEM FILAREE

Into November's brown yawn,
your perfect crimson intrusion
keeps flinging

Your pink rosettes
erode emptiness

Erodium, from the Greek
erodios, heron. Stork's bill,
crane's bill, redstem filaree

The shroud
of your red ruse

Of color

Of naming
what is here,
     without

What does the sky call you?

The sky calls me nothing.

CLOUD SEED, CONDENSATION NUCLEI, A GATHERING BILLOW

bends to near breaking. Bends to tear over summits,
lenticular, light arc against blue. No rain. The clouds
carry pastures and ponds and sutures. There is a rustle,
a slurry of grass and conjecture, some wind. No rain.
Already dust pirouettes, already the sun smarts, hints
of smoke, though just spring. Soon the unending days sifted with
ash, soon the black drape of ravens croaking of insidious soot.
But now the sky seems serene, amenable, full of redstarts.
They knit the breeze into stillness, then a turning over.

Clouds turning out. Matter turning out
to be named. Wind carrying the particulate, the heavy metals,
the VOCs, PAHs, an arc of toxic seep. Cloud seed. Condensation nuclei,
a gathering to billow, alveoli bend to near breaking. Our bodies
inflamed, who is at fault, blame ravens, pollen. The sky is blue,
our eyes are concave or convex, an arc asking. No rain. The clouds carry
suspensions, carry a mirror of poison and winsome selections
of the good shapes we remember as bucolic, benign. No rain.

A pulse of cumulus, stratus, nimbus, white over us. No rain.
Already the soil bleaches brown and cracks whip the dew, though night
still outlasts the day. Soon the redstarts will lose the hatch of light,
lose the clutch of branch where they left their brood. But now a few clouds
puff across a cadmium sky, a sky of phosphorus streaked with
lead. The air tastes of blood. The sky is
blue. No rain. What will cease this cycle, this lapse of knowing what's
enough, when every tongue's torn, burned over?
Cloud seed, condensation nuclei, a gathering billow.

All night I dream I hold clouds. With every movement I
sense the edges. I'm water, diving towards the center while my
body streams out, encircling. Always recollecting and dissipating around
condensation nuclei, cloud seed, my body the gathering billow.
Wind begins and gusts gesture between teeth and lips, phhhhhh, then
oxygen or vapor makes my iiiii, then my tongue finds
the roof with my jaw closing nnnnh. *Fine*. The sky is blue.
I can say these things, there is no poison, that the weather is fine.
But I can only speak with a mouthful of redstarts.

EVERY LEAF SWIFTING

I see a whirring stillness when a bee grazes my ear and I think *what makes sound become itself inside me when it is a wave only* but you see me as motion turning toward the bee sound, you don't know I'm looking at every leaf swifting, a scattering of invisible incisions, light refracting, something swirling, or finding the stoma of the alders and I have seen catkins first bursting in spring, but I can't speak of the memory with precision any more than I can explain the exact color blue that the rock doesn't keep but offers to me with the brush against vision we call perception, you inside your circuitous mind maze and I inside mine and together we feel the wind pulse and wonder for a moment about intention, what we can sense and grasp and what the wind can change direction for, and how it tastes to the birch or alder or lichen, or any stark stone.

LUXURIOUS EXCESS

tearing wings off the storm
this fever tree
        unverifiable

a logical scar
errant earth
                telescoped by the gush
we fail
              a tippy sun
says nothing
hovers over
        clotted water

uninformed stems inject petals

an opening
        proboscis into shadow
        hands move

touch failure

entangled in dark diatoms
these terrible staring sands

luminous quietude
shades of sustenance

insistent, evident
                  plastic
we fail
      tyrant needle

mystery severs
diminishing   symmetry

pollen
improvised sorrow

            as if photosynthesis
splits   our green sobs

UNHEALTHY FOR SENSITIVE GROUPS

the west
was the better of us
was the resin of night
was ferocious and domesticated

what clouds incorporated
into this uneven bloom
a translucent luxury
burnt slag to our lips

pollution as poultice
an inverse of vision
our incandescent jaws
stuck open and closed

desire was the adversary of us
was a tincture of dry fire
ambivalence neatly bilateral

DAYLIGHT SAVINGS

With sheer care they enter
and I learn to work the knife.
I holler for them to let me

in the swirled nest, toss stones
into the mock-whorl. Bees hover
over the tattered mantle, all

purple-blue tucked in cymes.
We circulate in vision-space.
The bees' drone plumps

folds, stuns pollen. We share
this expansive embrace and
an obsession with orbits.

From the resonant field, I tinker
with the solar angle. The bees
nearly tangle in shadow material.

An orange tinge twines their legs
and I shake to bend light. The stitch
of their hum tunes the prophetic clock.

In a parallel zone the sundial needs winding.

[ECOMELANCHOLIA IN SEA]

I learn to tell agates from quartz. Overqualified now to sort basalt from cement. Your cement my/our cemetery. If I were a grain of sand dollar I would only know flow/ no flow. Disturbance or / each essence. I would only feel the saturation of   [   ]. From halfway across   we share this and [earth death   ]   what cost   what cost Wait. Don't go. I could flash this water, bivalent across grass. Bivalent, back and forth, each drop drowns dry spaces. Oscillations become breaths. Mind holds agates by the

[   ]. Halfway   across a balance that is

AZIMUTH AND ALTITUDE FOR NORTHERN LATITUDES

Amber apex, motionless in sky, this light an axis for our
boreal blindness. The sun succumbs. Winter wills death to delicate green,
cedars stay. Seeds steel against ice, inch deeper in soil where
darkness decides. Cotyledons sleep in subterranean hope heaps. An
equilibrium of time mimed by tilt. Approach the horizon with precision
fixed star, wheel about awakening. Even with cold. Roots
geotropic, seep to ground, buried in frost. Evening a long slow tide of twilight, a
heliacal rising of paired planets. Moon moored, towards the azimuth of flight, the
irruptive flocks find seed. Grosbeaks, goldfinches, red crossbills in the glazed
june grass. Naked larch, sky the taste of winter, constellations flock in
kinnikinnick, evergreen arms color-spilled. Red berries snow buried. To see
light lapse into inky azure. The heat of sleep still seers the
moon. Slips beneath. Insolation, suspension of shadow in dark draws, pulls our
nuclei closer. Dimensionless expanse, a season of white wanders
ornate, blue flecked. Wind enkindles the crackling decay. Iridescence, sun dog,
parhelion, the ring of begin. Eyes open to everything, solemn shiver, the river
quartz-like, ice floes. Vitreous, viscous, encircles sky. Cliffs startle with white
radiance, water wanders below, nudges seeds. Ask the angle, when is it
summer with its verdant sepal swell? Purple petals into the press of
twilight's hand, let us remember the heated hymn of the green stagger. Exposed
under bare boughs, ochre culms, achenes rattle, yesterday's
vigor, seeds upon snow. Our hemisphere, this height, faces turned toward
wild anemia with molten want. It matters to be cold and alive, like a
xenocryst, internal clarity, though the fire's fled. Darkest day of the
year. Morning opens to an impoverished gray, a gradient of light, the
zenith angle. How we crave this pithy albedo, bright sun.

RED FLAG WARNING

when the plume bends
over us this way
its orange pink
belly grinds our eyes
with char

I dream of torrents
of muskegs in true night
ash filled hands
become sundews
bugs stick fast to hunger

in the morning
I taste red clouds
blackened woods

smoldering soil turns
into that day we rode swells
watched a raft of otters
colluvium spill into the bay

the fish flung their sea
slick bodies out into the fog
now we roil in smoke
sucking   gasping

otototoi black-backed woodpecker
how I hunger for that fresh wet air

MOUNTAIN BLUEBIRDS A LOCUS OF

Passing shadow passerine gather

                              wings

                                 unfold   flashing.

Call notes

      high   sweet   scattering

                              dissolute

                              on sage steppe.

We are agape
  water-full
  and found.

                Arriving again   blue
        wings   filling
                  turn from   form
                             circle
                             sharp angles
       the sleight of it.

Mesh of shadow.

    Shadow the straight sense   what's sought of it.

    Pulse contracting
  into spring-drenched sound.

                      Effluvium
                      of blue.

Bluebirds   followed by   following
    migratory   their bodies
                        our bearing.

Could we be kin   by what's shared   or

                          assured

           between us?

Our shadows   air-altered

                          cloaked & uncloaking

              buoyant

       held   here

             & soaring

STOP TO CONTEMPLATE
THE SHEER HEIGHT OF IT

the way wood shears

and masses at the base

notice how

pungent from cambium

everything

loses nothing

Are you

riveted by the

red-brown innards,

the banners of *Bryoria*,

the girth of grandeur

this fissured form?

These giant pines—

so much time

outside

with nothing

to prove

MORE BIRD MIND THAN SQUIRREL MIND

When squirrels
come to the suet,
I make my voice soft,
coo *squirrel, whatcha doing,*
and they squawk and dart
back to where they were,
an alley spruce behind
the house. Outside

birds tolerate me. One
chickadee on his flyway
from the feeder beaks a seed
and almost bounces off my face.

These juncos, chickadees,
house sparrows, house finches,
and sometimes nuthatches.

This cityscape, alleyway,
backyard refuge, greenstrip.

My alleyway is just private enough
that I can squat under the hawthorn
and pee on the earth.
I don't scare

them. The birds allow
this proximity. They can't see me

when my eyes
are closed.

BIVALVE

our humility or hesitation
chafes hemispheres
dips into the wrists
conceals the tense
succor sucker suckle
pulls seas from salt
diligence and glib labels
want water
ourselves (without)
trivial defects
of bleak simplicity

abrupt edges
stammer
document
disaster
earth breast
robs breaths
those people
tainted
verities
each trail
we walled

OUTSIDE, BY THE

I perceive gaps

between   awareness

                                                and when it isn't

green in some spots   blue in others

          we do not adhere to matter itself

                                                I saw an azure furrow
                                                breaking there in nonlocality
                                                as atoms in the sphere do

I spent all day watching an inchworm in dappled light

                              her hind legs anchored on snowberry
          she pivoted for purchase
                    continued abaxially

          I can't hear her   as she inches

                                                but the water, birds

this is not an approximation
                              of the leering cosmos

          there is a lineage of collapse   or

a giant benevolent machine

                    I go to the woods because I like the

CIVIL TWILIGHT

They ate everything— the black berries, sunflower seeds, the husk of my endoskeleton. When the day rang its singing bowl, it scared up a common green darner. The dragonfly landed and draped its iridescence onto my skin, doused us with blue ascension and red descent. In irregular intervals we slipped below the sensible horizon. Then the ascension and descent of avian bodies took up the rest of Sunday. I etched hieroglyphics on melted asphalt. A sickled sun breached totality, shed inky isotopes. My skin spun hungry. When the kinglets twined their claws around the golden currant, I asked them to pluck out my hard rind. The violet pith.

FLOURISH

conduit of peat   audible
then from the city's edge / coyotes'
wailing/ breaks on the wild hills   I
want to know if moss / these
feelings   all grow together   a

frass of ferns and hanging   / my
hands to your   green throat
when water   lets us up   from
this parched grasp   of   wet
longing   fickle sculpture

cups a tangle of green / calligraphy
bright shoots   names like *Bryum*
little leafbursts   a circlet
of intention / say   stairstep moss
say *Hylocomium splendens*   if

hands and knees / if dark and small
concentric zones   or   elaborate
etchings   gather / honor
fingers brush   a dearth of
barriers / say porous   pulse

NO ENTRY: A DICHOTOMOUS KEY TO ELEMENTAL DISARRAY

1a. My dome top is a viscid slick; ochre pores, gill-less..*Boletus edulis*

1b. Not as above 2

2a. When you mine my mind, mica smarts your lashing tongue 6

2b. I hold two hydrogens and an oxygen, unmarred 3

3a. Thorns adorn me, lichens splay from my grey limbs ....*Crataegus douglasii*

3b. My body is soft, or else the sharp parts are well-hidden 4

4a. When the Swainson's thrush calls I forget I have matter...5

4b. I pull myself up to summit tiny sky wounds 6

5a. Mouth stings of acid rain and/or leachate torques cells 8

5b. Not as above...11

6a. When the bees come I clutch them with blue-purple tubes ....*Penstemon* spp.

6b. When I feel my body I find just a few chloroplasts 7

7a. Scarred by a metal blow, my skin erupts from your pollen...............................*Phleum pratense*

7b. I tether an empty pause between anger and elation 8

8a. My yellow-white body feeds on scavenged sugars.................................*Corallorhiza trifida*

8b. Body green, inaudible, or otherwise fed.. 9

9a. Body glabrous, wax-white, or wanting.. 10

9b. Stem, leaves, and bracts with harsh stiff hairs ....*Castilleja hispida*

10a. Each raindrop spills sperm into my leaf labyrinth..............................*Polytrichum juniperinum*

10b. I taste a saline drought draped upon basalt 11

11a. You might believe cleaving matter is something other than assault............................ 12
11b. I push the button for colony collapse, listen for the last waning drone 13

12a. My trill: not a warning; my body, not a target..*Catharus guttatus*
12b. The air writhes with my protest; I shield ferns from your scythe............................. 13

13a. In the atomic blur we are monstrous, marred and gutting ....*Homo sapiens sapiens*
13b. I dream we're wise isotopes, a memory mass of gills ....*Homo sapiens sapiens*

33

LATER IN THIS SAME PASSAGE

after How Forests Think *by Eduardo Kohn*

A relational web although beginning.
Unpack the claim of some degree or other.

Fortunately wrong about emergent properties.
The event itself, and not just for the fact.

Precisely the proper significance specifies something about objects.
Relates differences.

Not just something. A convoluted process.
Signs. Being aware to enter the pattern.

The logic of attending to.
One might rightly say.

The very hierarchy, rather than, namely.
Organized around.

How to go about inhabiting.

Stable, fragile.
Fortunately wrong.

Another set of examples.
Nonspecific continuity.

We can all agree.
No one else, however, seemed to think.

When I say danger, I.
Only others snip this simplification.

Counterintuitively indifferent, dumb.
Distinctive attributes visible.

Values, by contrast intrinsic.

Symbols beyond our tendency.

FIELD NOTE: WE PONDER THE SIXTH EXTINCTION AT LEE METCALF WILDLIFE REFUGE

Our haven, this wildlife
refuge, is a sanctuary
for weeds and lead
ammo and dog crap.

Bohemian waxwings scatter
from the canopy, uncertain
whether hope is downstream
or upstream, or whether our bright ideas
choke the creek in every direction.

We find and admire
first spring flowers
sprung from piney debris:
Ranunculus glaberrimus
sagebrush buttercup.

Star moss, frog's pelt, pixie-cup
are whole here. In fifty years
when they ask will we offer
sensitive, threatened,
extirpated, extinct?

We watch trumpeter swans
dredge for snails
in the sky-hued slough.
Ripples move away
from their beaks,
radii spread.

At the edge of the river
cottonwood's blood-red
bud scales are splitting.

Resting here, our bodies
buoyed by puzzle bark,
we could almost forget
about imbalance.

TERPSICHOREAN

of what flows from the sigh
to spurn grown sand

of what flecks an obsidian din
from a stuck broke monsoon

now the dancing

ACROSS THE ICE SHELF, OMINOUS NEW RIFTS

Ice allocation   culls its listless blue

accelerating   spin

see   touched/untouched

unearthed   backbone of intent

leaden sprawl   another will

               what then?

no regard for wrens/robins

night-trussed   shadow

               hope's dark unravel

abandon   abrasion/reason

charm of aftermath

               uncertainty

roots draw/weld the moon

enter sullen state   enter

  forgotten cadence

    we heft   sky/scars

dissipation   loss

               what would it take?

voices   market our   unmaking

air engrained   viscous silt

soot-sewn   ourselves siloed

        sliver of   calving ice

tips an aura   boreal burial

glass resonates   blue

     our half-life   no   reason to?

water   other/other

an emerald erratic

       poison   poises

as immaterial   splendor

glacial elation   our exclusion

       matter into measure

terrain vague   emptiness

                    anatomy of melancholy
        undo unhappen unremember
affirms obliteration   landscape
        floating world   stuttering
kinetics   eyelid flip
            a dream of   flow
            facing us   facing   ice
hope of
                                    blank soil

MEANDER BELT

I knew there was going to be something because I have been watching. We get there by walking. We have been watching and knowing and I knew it was going to be something. Not today not that again, not that old thing with the choke-stacked air already catching in the throat, tang of toxin, fixed tangent. Not today no today we just do flowers. We love the flowers and lichens under bunchgrass shadows and watch red velvet mites motor through leaf litter. Today no motors but the roar of the jet and the jerk of the truck pulling us up dirt draws. Up the draws and over we see coyotes and sand hill cranes and the tuft of *Bryoria* we find on the ground where the land folds itself over into extended shadow. We get there by walking, we see what there is and keep walking and all around us miles of blue and green and brown. We are higher than the trees. We are higher than the trees and down below in Tongue Creek a cow elk comes out of the cottonwoods and moves through. How do we move through. Move through that old thing. Subduction zone on the edge of serration. Not that again. Walking we knew we would find certain things but not *Bryoria* on the edge of *Ochrolechia*, brown wiry tuft coming out of those apos. We were walking and we stopped and we were watching and there it was that lichen. Just spilling brown and angling up and moving through.

DID THEY ASK

I find you still
but singing
midway up
the snag

one thrush
on an unwavering
spire

two notes

then you are
quiet
I am quiet too

across the canopy
others sing to you

your kind

a hummingbird
draws drums
from motion

a ruby-crowned kinglet
carries air into
oscillation

do they hear us
sing you, and why

a cassin's vireo asks
and asks and
asks

here I am
where are you:

you?

OF PARADOX

Regardless of intention, what will build and build. Events accumulate between us, tangible. A hand unmarred. What about your first movement, or my last? What of the black asking? Unrelenting irregularity. Verisimilitude. Frenetic excision. I remember standing in front of the picture. What anyone thinks, I don't remember ever after.

— — —

A scrape of chair or is it a log truck taking the last of the trees. A banging chair or door above the buzz of florescence but I want inflorescence so I hear nothing anymore. I can nearly not exist; all of me is enveloped by atoms that sip at my seams. Energy between the chair and my backside is the same because I am still. All except a pull of air, I exist as cavern with a movement of grass and a tidal tug of enclosed air where no one else moves mostly. I am not afraid to not exist. I am not afraid to remember how I am a number of stacked cells, that I can enumerate emptiness or create but I won't push it past, won't insist on it, won't fill my mind when I can ease into the seam.

— — —

I dismiss a sense of ongoingness. Does water deform the air? Reminiscence lacks insistence but I thought I knew your face. When we shook hands I left mine there as a retainer, as in what tissue could attain inside your palm. No business there, inhabiting us like that. The sun with its endless embeddedness. All interiority empties out when we sleep. It goes on and on. Stuck stick drip drip sunk. Tick tock grip fast first. Of ample ardor. Elaborated. Actualized. Attempted whenever possible. Does matter. Flit. Threshold.

— — —

Reverse engineering. Mental soil, entropy. Cup cis-trans cistern half held. Lucid critter. Ozone layer refilling with ozone. Pencil going dull. Plastic to dissolve. Milk to sour. Awaken. Awaken awaken awaken, and pour.

— — —

Was I alone? Was I witness to the seasons? Was the cement crumbling?

— — —

Spindly insides the size of stories, his story her story hearsay, heresy, chiasma of mouths enfolding. Past becomes homogeneous, all of it there newly untouchable. Consider the distance, consider the linearity of extraction.

— — —

Generous, this homogeneous sky, this continuum of blue. How the flicker encounters air and its elements, the pictoral tilt, ensnared. He finds the stovepipe, perches on its silver stilts and pecks. The rattle reverbs, tattles tales of its mate march. It's February and broods and broods will soon ensue.

— — —

When the pendulum parted and edged open the area apart took on the weight of geometry. The angle that sustained it, the half wrought half hidden argument of ordering, eliminating the gradation of reality that exists only with extension into anything, stopped. The material of measure became ardor and absence, language and light.

— — —

There was a dream spilled on textiles and soon the only sound was a million microbes metabolizing. Who says microbes can't speak, or swallow, as each lyric was lost. What followed was emptiness, and the pieces that stayed were the ones that no one wanted to eat, allow, or order.

— — —

My head struck a water well, and lost the sound of certain,
I drank a drip, of time to lip, then memory returned uncurtained.

— — —

Mirroring feet moving to touch, skin of remembering. Cells intrinsically breathing together, same inscriptions and membranes, motion and interval. Same blood. Sameness not in name, language a near lack, but similitude, mother and daughter, two conglomerations emulating matter, and other.

— — —

Let it stop here with the poison arrow pulled back. Sand hill crane refrain. Is that where the spiral stops. Between when. Golgi body glows. Actual hour a small swap. Loose minutes a slight puppet. Rescue curfew curlew what to mention, mask the mess of.

— — —

Four petals mean mustard, five implies endless inclusion into tribes and clades. Four petals can mean native, or exotic, an elegance, or a scourge. Petioles and leaves may have hairs, simple or stellate. Four petals may mean monster, or miracle.

— — —

See this is her nature, the ravaged wreckage, the aftertrash, here, her burden, this air, her soiled stare.

— — —

Already outward. Agglomeration of will and want and excess, flashing. Did I ask it. Already becoming. Already stops within it. Already dissolves into differentiation. Turns into. Sown.

MEANDER BELT

VISCOUS SLICK

Like an eternal surge of epinephrine, it quickens
        (inters reverberations)
An electron cloud roils, is this aggregate of asphalt
        (buries lacunae, porous dirt, clods of moss)
Our chloroplasts spindle
        (periodic table unravels)
DNA splits, is darned into kinetic impotence
        (base pairs cleave)
Tell me— what is the half-life of empathy?
Dark frolic (tar teeth) our lurch of dust

THE WARMING

All night the halted echo
of a barred owl skims

pines. The trees
squirm with wind.

And my mind—
restless with earth death.

The throat of drift
charms morning. Siskins

sing their upturned
zéee-eee, and we turn our

scurry towards sun-
streaked wings. Whenever

their song stirs, it blooms
clean, a honey-plume.

What about their blunt hope?
Life arises from incoherence.

Such particular tumult of
greening and growing, and my

body pale and still. Pivot of
inaccessible wing. These raw

rungs cue the barred
owl. Our obscure cure

for voicelessness
burrs a warning.

We scry our abyss,
warm, rhythmic.

I STARTED EATING ROSE PETALS

only in the woods.
It feels barbaric
to have petals
stuck in my incisors.

I mean you wouldn't
eat ornate adornments
of animal sex organs?
No. You would not.

Still, they are sweet
and their fragrance
bathes my tongue.
I am a rough brute.

ON CRUSTOSE LICHENS

Nose to ground, knees near nose, belly folding over. Stoop to see life. Lichens. Two unlike things meld, become one. All colors, all kinds, like an endless soil skin. What if you look close? Closer. Bumpy white body flecked with black sex sacs. Those are the apothecia. Slice a little under the scope to see spores.

Crustose, foliose, suppose you knew their language. Suppose you always see the sky.

AIR QUALITY INDEX

torrential sky and smoke
an acid tongue lashing
across the sheen of crisp fields
was it only yesterday
we were sun hungry—
don't touch me now
this is between me
and the rain

TO GATHER NECTAR

I see liquid trees above me, they
drip pitch in my xylem spine.

I see a drab black lack,
a fire licking broken ash.

I hear the ground, sand, green
and brown grains sifting down.

I see a lobe of cloud drop pollen
into an illusion of horizon.

I see circles slip into stone
wing sewn, strewn with sun.

I see a ruby-throated thrum hovering,
half-hidden in a moat of crimson.

I hear something striking, a
flint of chert, or bone, splitting.

I see a wild shred of woods, a singular
angle, a small spit of splendor.

I see sedges twist, spring flecked and
wind inscribed, filled with night.

I enter an alluvial altar where
herons sieve the sea, breath by breath.

Look at these trees leaking salt, eyes
squeeze shut when waves spray.

Look at the anemone open to
the sea, arms stung with longing.

But what will write this body,
this gathering of nectar, this newness?

Listen, listen, listen. I sip
suchness between thorns.

SURROUNDING THE SENSES

after The Spell of the Sensuous *by David Abram*

As long as the rain
as long as the reverberation
isn't verbal a very bare
sound goes down by the
river and washes its vowels off.

Echo
the things, their own tones and textures.
Climb down the pattern
where vision snags on
something other than other.
Is an offering.

The sum of assertions says something
blue or black or born whirling
is a mirror that goes by many names.
None of them begin with a
or end in zenith.

The sensible world wants words, but the wind
within it isn't uttering. The bulk of
jagged snags dissipates into uncivilized
oblivion.

Primordial awareness incarnate carves
colors from us. Sooner or later the
contours count, sooner or later
pivotal magic.

MARKINGS CRISP AND VARIABLE

Three dark-eyed juncos
hover over snow.

The first junco, a swell and bulge of meltwater
is undecipherable before the drip. Lines

of clear obscurity sluice the far reach
of vision. The second junco is a four-merous

atrium holding equal volumes of
ocean. The ventricles slip open, emit light.

Between air and ocean lies the septum, sutured
with sound. The third junco, wet from the sea,

arises from cotyledons. Green holds
clasp the stem, cells become lingual.

They open and close
their stomata to practice speech

try out words like alluvial
and loss. Three dark-eyed juncos

peck the crisp seeds from fall.
When their beaks part, I tumble in

clutching the bole of a redwood tree
a snailshell, and half a blue-green sash.

AUTUMN HYMN

after Karen Volkman

The elision of hours decants without.
Blinding brilliance, hyperspectral bloom
chisels clouds to sheer static spume.
An integral bliss brims the day stout,

fractures the frailty filled with doubt.
Great heights hold hues, a blue limned womb
vertiginous in the void, auspicious plume.
And presence is the clarity with clout.

It is insistent. Fractal flowers flay
the sky, a cadence of afference. Achenes,
potent with promise, fulgency fled,

find cerulean spirals, windward led.
How wide the blunt blue day, unforeseen,
latent with life, this autumnal dream.

EVEN AS WE APPROACH IT

Holding up stones, blue lines layered, pollen-limned.
Calling you here, wild ginger light

on my tongue. Riffles fold white over green, the river
dismantles distance between us, pours your face into

my open hands. What fluidity finds. Amalgamation of
intention and desire and alluvium. Hyphenated sun slips

closer. Cottonwood seed rain, between
caddis flies and kingfishers and willows. Something

to walk out on. With one side a medium for impermanence,
how can it stay? Wren song. The moment when touch becomes

shadow. High water line, where color grains shift. A fritillary lands,
unfurls its tongue. Not the way I would have imagined, not uncoiling.

A loosening. To not hold so tightly. Two swallowtails meet
midflight and swirl together, fall. Into the river of your eyes,

asking. Could you hold this fullness? A small swarm of wings
hover over wet sand. You, calling me here, emerge

breathless. If desire curves out like an echo, would we entwine.
Striders slip across the indigo deep. Viscosity holds our bodies, shared

breaths. Lures liquidity. Into what will follow. Did you see
the fish jump? All I saw were waves, water parting.

NOTES FROM THE CENTER OF A GLACIAL LAKE

If I escape feetward, I'll shed demise like a virus. You're all vaccine to me now, failed promise, a malaise of progress, modernity, filth. Take this all back. Take your radioactive half-lives, hexane from my water, malignant dead zones. Take them. I leave this body where it fell, here in the water, where I start this important study of physics and color and light. Somehow I stay upright. Somehow all this water moves beneath me and I'm unwavering in intersections of viscosity. Sometimes cerulean slips down the lee side, and gray flips sunward. Sometimes brilliance fixes itself on fleeting peaks. Your clouds are brown, hysterical, but here I'll pretend they're unbeaten, pristine. I'll become an unbidden rivulet. You can remember me not a body, not brokenhearted, just liquid, just this skirl of light.

ALASKA TELL ME THERE'S SOMEWHERE SAFE FROM US

Your ferns' murmur tugs
my umbilicus, fierce wilderness.
My black-hole heart is wrung
with excess. Let me hear your air chafe

trees, frenzied ocean of fringed light
cup muskegs. Your insides
are plumbed, a black slick.
Your swans, stung with frost

carbon rings and dust. So let
me be your nothing, a lick of bark,
a fire in your molten belly, fervent
bent of your archipelago, stark.

FUZZY TONGUE PENSTEMON

White witness to fluked
shadow, stamens arc
like bones. From across the vast
grass, wind tide brings a swarm
of bees. A series of swerves
admits no coincidence.
The blue petals hold
what they want, and only
bees brush up to those
bowed white trusses.
When they leave, they leave
the flowers empty,
as if excising pale dread
from the face of us.

WHAT SIFTS THE STRAITS
OF THIS PEBBLED TREBLE?

Ethereal mineral
oscillates, sifts.

Hues construe what
waves imbue, this

illogical illusion,
liquid eclipsed.

Even in symmetry,
the dew drop slips.

WE WENT UP MT. BALDY TO BOTANIZE AND GRAY FOG

flew upslope, sheared the valley. Wind waned sound. Someone said *look at this gilia,* someone said *I feel I'm in an airplane,* and someone said nothing and sat to watch the invisible view. A hermit thrush trilled. Eyes followed pitch-perfect flowers, color excess, shuddering culms. Through a small sun-scathed hole the horizon emerged. From here we couldn't see the river or the torn ground. Only a gray scarcity of scars. From both sides the storm sought itself and the clouds closed. Someone said *maybe we should leave the mountain,* someone said *it's just fog,* and someone said nothing and sat between songbirds. Hail fell, first halting, then touched each leaf level with sky.

EVEN THOUGH, USNESS

empty nest ( )
and I shouldn't
care whether nature
succeeds, even

though (usness (
I'm of it and for it
and arguably
from it

the robins' nest—
markless
the nestlings ( )
absent—

wild optimism
wild empathy
        (ours (

this time success
this time (usness (
we bleed empty ( )
nurtured even

(I HEAR)[6] (TOO MUCH)[7]

Too much metal brushed up against memory, ripples from the Eocene. I hear air tastes like sound and plaits smell from the swollen marsh. Too many shadows and waves then the plates move. I hear the brown earth's stomach's hungry. Too many pocks of poison. I heard that from a thrush. Too many times to count erasure by lidded men. I hear the other half of hatred is nothing that can be broken, is its wake. Too much orchestration of torture. I hear touch is the seek of smeared ultramarine. Too much plastic palette. I hear a splinter of metal quiver; I mime thorns. Too much brine from stone.

SOIL, RE-VISITED

The undrawn slough of winter exhales.
On southern hills the snow subsides, the flattened
remnant of summer's husk. The grass culms unveil
meniscus of consequence. A jaded dream to tend.

Adornments empty into tinned and pale
drums, beating. Petals an apparition, suggestion
of falling latitude. Was this our idea, this gale
of green effaced? Even the coppered litter stuns

us, even the rain. Winter hid the dead slag river
and hid the gush. Now the seasonal refrain.
The mouths that open mime disaster. A shiver,
a spate of dirt, a froth of methane, disdain

for natural. The compass needle errs. It drones
of stasis, is nothing like our chime of bones.

WE LEFT TO LET THEM STEW IN THEIR PREDICAMENT

Irradiated gaze, the wolverine stops within feet of me. Eyes me.
The derivative of noiselessness roils between us. Amoeboid
clouds hover over ozone holes. Who am I to know this animal.
The instant pivots sharply to fill the cavern with more
than the known whole. They always seek me they find me
open and listening. In an eternal moment the mind is subsumed
by the indispensible condition. She tucks me in her lope, my arms
clasp her brown gait. I dredge snow, glacier lilies, and trilliums.
The sky is peevish and the forest peevish but somehow lavish. I shed
my false density in the yew and hold fast. Lashed to brisk vision,
she derides the ultimate. I find the cedar trees intact, the creek
still moving. My body no longer holds me and I spill out there
among the argillite. In the thick of the giant correction crises clot
sufficiently grey. Why does she come so close. We find estrangement
in tangibles, the perennial question of encounter. Why does she look at me
like that. The lance of storm gnashes its groan across the wilderness
cracked and browned. In memoriam, in memoriam, cheap resources
pile like swag. She could rip me open with those claws before
I uncap the spray. What is left to empty. Everything since has been built
with falseness. Eyes me, eyeing I. Consider Pleiades, responsible
and traceable materials, products astrally astray. Consider darkness
no longer the body that smothers us.

PERIGYNIUM

My black throat parts, loon song.
I call to you, call to you,
like I've never seen the end
of water. Hands slight to drift.
Loon song, ululation, echo.
An evolution. I want to,
want to, our.

FIND THE FOCI

An unclasped lapse
an ascent slips into

                our axis, to wonder   what if
                 the fourth breath was the fifth?

A sharp breach of shadow
red-tipped

                      our arrow
                          such fissures.

      If:

matter is stark

                      and
                      each edge is chert
                        drought fraught

                  and

epithelia is pith

      then
      would cells instill

             this ellipse?

VALENTINE

if flowers were a symphony
violets would be a xylophone
or maybe the vibes
if it were a jazzy spring

GENERAL EVIDENCE

after Call Me Ishmael *by Charles Olson*

Interested in beginnings, I take space to be ancient fact plus a harshness.

Prophecies seek cold,   combustion yields
     the precision instrument.   Blue as baleen.

   Those deep faraway things flash forth.

Breath, the only necessary ecology. Such reality, fixed blackness.

     Stir in torment.   Abrupt.   Inimical.

I stumbled when I saw it.   See her as object, or velocity.
Symbol of *has its way, soft.*

     A quantity lies flat.

I measure the thing, the whole persistent multitude.   *Bewildered*

and confounded with the din, the labyrinth, the barbaric confusion of the whole.

    As it is built with.   As it is rubble.

A long slope of crags   rocks gnawed and mumbled   no moss.

   It all finally has to do with denial.

A last fact,   confirmation of margin we still fail to measure.

Now come to the inmost leaf of the bulb.

FUNERARY

This ambiguous orbit starts
        somewhere between
the second and third touch
of a carnivorous clutch.

        We follow the moving eye of shadow
        drawn black across unfaltering gasps.

Mountains darn a clot
of fog, are a current of
want.

The saline rise of not good enough
this toxic spit of indifference.

        A fragrance of rust
        fecundity of absence.

These spindles were hands.

        Beyond the floral orbit no bees. A smear
        of cement, some blind drone.

The collapsible web:
        collapsing.

        Attention—aster   attention—ash

forget this false order, the irresistible instability of entropy
        more or less crushing.

Each insect is pinned
each limb chloroformed,
pallor plucked from herons'
drastic movements,
a plummetous
descent.

       Dismiss this.

No spatial detail
warrants   delusion.

Fault lines were sliding under.
We mistook this incision for insight.

THE GARDEN OF SURGING WAVES IS A SQUARE

With a wall of rusty words, though
You'd have to stand in the hole
Of the empty lot to read them.
My daughter is bored in the Garden

Of Surging Waves. I run my hands along
Marble columns carved with animals
And plants no one remembers.
Few plants are alive in the garden.

We know this place to be Astoria not
Portland because there are no homeless
Sleeping in the garden. We left
Our home to wander in the garden

Because here there's no smoke. This place
Is fresh but would swell with ocean
If the Cascadia Fault goes. We don't talk
about that though, not future disasters

Only the ones we can outrun.

O STUNNED MOUNTAINS
OUR SHAME

after From Sand Creek *by Simon J. Ortiz*

flowers bleed
breath
  shatters
this iron river

opened with
salvation   generations
mountains

dew reassures
or crosses
splits eternity

       remembers
blood   or freedom
 or   plenty

this train rode sighs
drowning
finality   mangling
who

exculpate stares
stunned   in justice
rise to
embrace   arise

the smallest conceit
culled from
us them
      thunder

RIPARIAN REPARATION

I watch a great blue heron
an aria blisters in my throat
what calls for the shrouding
for colors to close

leaves curls inward
leaves curls outward
and somewhere lies the swoon

once I was city stuck
struck deaf to darkness
before I knew sky as a smear
of river, dilute

stones do not waver, only swerve
with the perception of motion

consider the stubborn elements
wild surrogate for none

FIRST SHAPELESS

Drawn from darkness and absence
all the roots bring something, even

at the edge of synthesis. Matter is a live flux
of forgotten fury. You can learn to fathom motion.

Wake to see a spill of spores sway with wind
haloed and frenzied. Every moment your pinnate

nature streams from you cytoplasmic, a cataclysm
of propriety and piety. And why not.

Today clouds stall, split like the land, and for
a second you think that's it, even vapor succumbed

to human numbness. But your hand moves back
to the page, readies ink and disperses desire

the whole of you still wild, with only thought
cut up in its detriment. Optimism is colorless

no longer spare. Hope sticks like a watermark,
no memory of expression, green spreading

like a soft utterance, first scalpeled smooth, then
becoming a deciduous tempest. One perfect petiole

cupped pulsing in your empty palm.

TRIMEROUS

RED-BREASTED NUTHATCH

Whose tongue? Infinite affinity,
cup of the other, this
refugium. Became a voice

PELTIGERA VENOSA

When sun stung,
awaiting water, lichens
dissipate light. Could we

FRITILLARY

The whole winter waiting. If
blossoms slip from longing,
these petals are a pulse.

GLACIER LILY

How signals sort creation
This destining of being
What the forest knows

MITELLA

Little *Mitella,*
mineral green pool—
the secrets seeps keep

HAWTHORN

New leaf mother one spring
came home hopeful, hopefully
year after year. Is thorned

GILIA

Enframing diversity
A scarcity of scarring
This wild we welcome

OWL'S CLOVER

From underneath the umbra
no mind, no owl, no stance
bursts this umber puncture

ALLIUM

Color excess, soil spill
bud-filled, forgotten.
The start of its skin

PRAIRIE CONEFLOWER

Near specific apices
elapsing past clasp:
meadow know-how

BEE BALM AND SWALLOWTAIL

Not sweet this time, not neatly
Or in order, not anything
We've touched before

BLANKETFLOWER

If the tilled tide is curling
I don't want there to be
less of you

LESS, UNLESS

SKY-PAUSE

Existential exit, take the first left at the larch, past three peltigeras, until you get to the sedge edged alluvium. Hold stones until your skin becomes mineral.

To rescind the sentiment of spilling would be to silence sentience. A volume of melody domes dim if the leaves sieve close. There is still time to learn how to listen.

She imagines she's a newscaster. There are only 35,524 animals left in the wild and populations are declining. There is a book robber and he robbed all the books

and the world won't ever be the same. *Is there any good news.* Yes, we have a lot of information on the robbers. We know so much. We have so many details.

Falter flat, fate, flit and fly. Do I have to. For if fear and effort fret, fault fate. Do you. Bereft rift, fire fib. Are you listening. Sinister cinder incends cistern. Does it burn.

Thinking of her again, the child who walks in the waste and finds phosphorous. The chickadee finds birdseed, tap tap tap. How do you feel today, chick-a-dee-dee-dee.

Lying in change loosely losing light. Swimming in embryonic intricacy. Telos. A becoming. Everything inherent, resplendent, plentiful, sunk. Under waves, waiting.

Are you broken? *Not me.* Someone. *Is it you?* She reads a book on scarcity. *Ask me about it.* What is scarcity? As if this needs to be taught.

I do this so when I dance flowers fly from my fingers. There is no other way to find the stratosphere. Short of spearing skeins of sky. Do I want this.

Thank you for this earth. Let's eat. Please pass the pine pulp. Did you get enough of these mashed trees? Seconds on herons, please. My, this mountaintop is delicious.

We found our way out through a tear in the bark. It led to a land where beings bartered for a fiercer berator, an orator of torture. We returned to the tree, unseen.

The voices said it was so, and so and so said it was the voices. So it's spun. Someone says we're so sorry. So is the sky. So are you. So sad, so sorry. So they say.

You could climb if you want to but the limbs aren't low. You know the sounds and the smells and how to tell if it's morning. No meaning, no moaning, no mourning.

Palpable probable, implorable. Unbearable, unstoppable, affordable. Treatable, toilable, tearable. Inflatable, irritable, illegible. As you found it.

There is no way out of this flower. We are eager to find the edge but fringed petals leave us upended. We feel the slippage of light, but sky evades us. We return to root.

The ousel is the only bird she can remember. The rest have been erased. It is considered a great success. Although she stands by the creek and dips all day.

I want this meadow to be more to you than charmingly miscellaneous. I learned each plant here and I don't find it dauntingly difficult. I find the assemblage absolute.

A review of the universe will be held at six o'clock. If you miss it be prepared to walk this hilltop through space's rapport of sun, earth, moon, and all the constellations.

After the caddis hatch, swallows swoop over the river. Their motion reminds me of forever. Not in the knowable way, but in the way rivers smell like remembering.

The stones are a seep between tepal-speak. They slip between loose layers of air, the strata of errata you left when you decided nature wasn't worth listening to.

At the edge of Belonging you asked me if I would go in with you. The people there were wearing too many clothes and pinching paunches. I stayed in Other-Ether.

Between your ease and the trees' *please* no one felt comfortable. There was no sign of the eraser. Those things will stay. They want. The tree excused itself, and I followed.

The atlas is to last as parse is to past. The face is to farce as gape is to gasp. The whole is to whirl as friend is to find. The mark is to make as mend is to mind.

Orange blossoms respire nectar and it is a barrier to progress. This will not be tolerated. Committees delegating destruction have been formed. Final notice.

Do you want to understand. Do you want to hold the half of water, wander in its ether. Do you want to build mud castles and see the sun's whole heat. Do you dream.

Permission to speak for the flowers. Permission to spill from the hours. Permission to hang from the bowers. Permission to sneak past the scowlers. Foul fabler! Tabled.

On a large scale it promotes infiltration. It waits for days without water, no stems to speak of. Its little leaves are a favorite of one small girl. She says *I heart moss.*

When it landed on the loon and cantered on raccoons, time slanted. In the space that ensued, no money was due, for money was extinct and supplanted.

Inspiration: *Act of drawing in, especially inhalation of air into the lungs. Excitement of the mind or emotion to a high level of feeling or activity.* Is breath enough.

Underneath latent earth, a sense of soil. There is no argument. Leaves live, die, the soil seeps black. More life. Then enters our delirium of destruction.

We slept in the snow to get an early start. The volcano had already blown its top and we wanted to see inside. Halfway up we were snow mired. No matter, kind summit.

Its laughter and its learning are unwitting to itself. It wants to know what it is here for. We are in the final stages of testing. When released it will want to see the sky.

The illusion of the conclusion is the incision of the mind. A suspicion of perdition is what prayers hide behind. The ruse of the news—no one's immune to earth-death blues.

Sullen moon, why won't you stay. Hear us calling from the dark places. It is impossible to untangle these vines without you. Even when we use our will.

The edge of the ultramarine iris runs over dark rocks. The petals all have powers and they sew sentences from the mouths of monsters. We speak in sepals.

It shows little resistance to disturbance. Its resilience is not its brilliance but its bane. We stepped on it again and it's gone. Ding-dong, earth is dead.

The distillation of original air went off to find fair origin. When it got to the sea
it cried this can't be, for the ocean had sublimed into fortune.

I don't want to know if you killed it. I don't want to know if you did it was it you.
It was good in my stomach, it was good when we were laughing, are we good.

Watching the way waxwings cluster and split, fill the air with matter. You and I are half
buoyant. A will is illuminated. We practice the feeling of falling before flying.

Get yourself some chlorophyll a, b, and c. Put it in your body: vegetarian alimentary.
Get some muscle cells, we call it meat. Put it in your body, that's how carnivores eat.

Sandstone walls, narrow and mica-flecked. We are never where we started, or where we
wanted to be. But here the blue that finds us, finds us belonging.

The stars bring many feelings. Water brings many feelings. The sky brings many feelings.
Rocks bring many feelings. I don't bring any as I forgot to stop at the store.

The tactile tic of a woodpecker's beak wakes us. We have become variations of flint and
flourish. Apart strikes the strength of unknowing. As in, what we could sing for.

Forget the eclipse, the little sliver that slips past your lip into smile. Forget the scarlet
spire that carries a crisp rasp of crows. Forget to follow. Grow forceful.

Stasis, we love it when you work those feedback loops. We run amuck but you return us
to the middle. There is no danger of careening. We like how you change us.

The elk chews the chaff grips the calf. The bat sips the sweets sucks the fruits.
That bird parts the pitch flips the midge. This bird sinks the skink misses moss.

Intersecting sectioning, intercepting imperceptibility, interacting: is centering.
Day and night and day and night and day and night and day and night. And day.

I see my hands hold questions, twining into thought. I see my house holds items, the
things I've bought. If all is mere matter, no worse is the latter, for that is just taught.

It's good enough, leave it how you found it just leave. It's healthy enough, we're healthy enough just breathe. Don't speak of it don't think of it, don't seek it, it's gone.

I recognize the lichens on my solstice tree. *Usnea, Bryoria, Melanohalea, Hypogymnia, Parmelia.* I hastened their earth-death. Is loving them enough.

Carmine, vermillion, cerulean hue. Burnt umber, scarlet, Prussian blue. Ochre, pear, Parnassian green. When evening falls all colors climb back in. I am color so I follow.

Running at the ocean at night is like falling into a heron's body and lunging at the sun. The roar rakes our fear into elation and also takes our clothes. We swim.

When hence twilight met mighty twill, darkness danced, half-harkened its will. It said let me stay, but light hastened away, and the bleakness of blackness instilled.

Today the branches know no stillness. They make small circles, moving from where they begin to every way they can bend. I feel my fingers become pliant.

Perplexed explanations masked excisions of axillary allowance. Hollow calyx asked for exact caskets of light. A palate of pale parcels sung in season. All was expected.

The trees bind my eyes. When I start to move I find sky in my mouth. Sometimes twigs touch far reaches, a sensing. I can't ignore the feel of flying. I can't ignore this reach.

The living things have already packed. There was a lottery and lichens drew first. They will be joined by chickadees and thrushes. I forgot to buy a ticket so I'll stay.

Put it in the xylem and put it in the phloem. Put it in the clouds and put it in the fen. Put it in our bodies as if we like it too. Don't call it toxic or poison, call it residue.

The insects know the bottom of the flower as Sky-Pause. The space between the petals they call Allowable Air. When I ask what they call us they just laugh and point.

A wolverine pierced my human fable and all my myths leaked out. All I could do was stare at water. I tried to splint the wound with words, but wind kept getting in.

NOTES

Italics in "Into the Birdless Ether" and the first epigraph are from Timothy Morton's *Hyperobjects: Philosophy and Ecology After the End of the World*.

The second epigraph is from Juliana Spahr's "Calling You Here" in *That Winter the Wolf Came*.

ACKNOWLEDGMENTS

"Cloud Seed, Condensation Nuclei, a Gathering Billow" appeared in the Riverfeet Press anthology *Awake in the World*, 2017.

"Funerary" appeared in *Epiphany Magazine*, 2017 and was nominated for a Pushcart Prize.

"Find the Foci", "Surrounding the Senses", and "Imagine Being Present And Finding Yourself Gone" appeared in *Mud Season Review*, 2017.

"I'm Ready to Tell You about the Bodies" appeared in *Pilgrimage Magazine*, 2017.

"First Shapeless" appeared in *Meniscus*, 2017.

"Ecomelancholia in Sea" and "Mountain Bluebird a Locus of" appeared in the Open Country Press anthology *Bright Bones: Contemporary Montana Writing*, 2018.

"Meander Belt", "Even as We Approach It", and "To Gather Nectar" appeared in *Mantis* 2018.

"No Entry: A Dichotomous Key to Elemental Disarray" appeared in *Cold Mountain Review*, Spring/Summer 2019.

ABOUT THE AUTHOR

Rebecca A. Durham is a poet, botanist, and artist. Originally from the Connecticut River Valley of New England, she also calls Montana home. She holds a BA in Biology from Colby College, a MS in Botany from Oregon State University, and an MFA in Creative Writing (Poetry) from the University of Montana. Nominated for a Pushcart Prize, Rebecca's writing has been featured in national and international journals, literary magazines, and anthologies. As a botanist, she has worked across the west exploring ecosystems. She lives with her daughter in Missoula, MT. More about her work can be found at rebeccadurham.net.

ABOUT NEW RIVERS PRESS

New Rivers Press emerged from a drafty Massachusetts barn in winter 1968. Intent on publishing work by new and emerging poets, founder C.W. "Bill" Truesdale labored for weeks over an old Chandler & Price letterpress to publish three hundred fifty copies of Margaret Randall's collection *So Many Rooms Has a House but One Roof.* About four hundred titles later, New Rivers is now a nonprofit learning press, based since 2001 at Minnesota State University Moorhead. Charles Baxter, one of the first authors with New Rivers, calls the press "the hidden backbone of the American literary tradition."

As a learning press, New Rivers guides student editors, designers, writers, and filmmakers through the various processes involved in selecting, editing, designing, publishing, and distributing literary books. In working, learning, and interning with New Rivers Press, students gain integral real-world knowledge that they bring with them into the publishing workforce at positions with publishers across the country, or to begin their own small presses and literary magazines.

Please visit our website: newriverspress.com for more information.